Real Estate
Creative Financing

Bruce Kellogg

PAGE PUBLISHING
Conneaut Lake, PA

First originally published by Page Publishing 2024

ISBN 979-8-89157-263-8 (pbk)
ISBN 979-8-89157-278-2 (digital)

Printed in the United States of America

Contents

Introduction

Beyond Cash

Traditional financing

Traditional home financing in the United States is a cash down payment to the origination of a new loan. Commercial properties are purchased in much the same way. The key is the employment of cash.

The other way: Creative financing

This book is intended to be a thorough guide to investing using alternatives to cash. It's known as creative financing, and you will learn all about it here. We will be going way beyond cash.

Case no. 1. Suppose I owned a duplex, and an identical duplex was run down next door. I found the owner was an anesthesiologist who lived 60 miles away. He admitted that he never visited his property or maintained it. I offered him a) zero down payment; b) a 20-year loan with no interest, just principal-only payments; c) payments equal to the rents he was receiving; d) paying his closing costs for him. Win-win? You bet! He took it!

Case no. 2. A family in our circle decided to relocate to the foothills of the Sierra Mountains. They owned two tract homes locally as rentals. I offered to buy them subject to the existing first loans and take out a second loan with them for their equity. The husband wanted a down payment of an unfinished, new rolltop desk from a local furniture store. I put the desk on a VISA credit card and paid their closing costs, and the houses were mine. No cash down payment. Seller financing. Win-win.

Case no. 3. For a time, I was part of a group of real estate wheeler dealers, where real and personal properties were traded around. My favorite trade I saw was a mid-1930s 42-foot motor yacht with an inboard 350-cubic-inch Chevrolet engine used as a down payment on an 8-unit apartment building. The yacht was all wood, and the interior appointments were stunning. It was regal!

The cases cited above are meant to introduce creative financing and to whet your appetite for it. It's fun! It's creative! It's lucrative! And you'll meet some real characters along the way. So let's go!

Chapter 1

Notes and Security Instruments

Getting started

Any extensive presentation of creative financing necessarily begins with notes and their security instruments. Notes are promises to pay money from one party, the payor, to another, the payee. They have been around in various forms for centuries, and their use is highly refined at this point. Let's discuss the three main types.

Figure 1

PROMISORY NOTE—UNSECURED

Prepared by: Agent_________________________ Phone_________________________

Broker_________________________ Email_________________________

NOTE: This form is used by a loan broker or escrow officer when originating an unsecured loan or seller extension of credit to a buyer without a trust deed lien on real estate to evidence the debt owed and the terms for payment.

DATE: ______________, 20________, at _________________________, California.
Items left blank or unchecked are not applicable.

FACTS:

1. On or before ____________, 20______, without a grace period, or ______ on demand,

    1.1. ____, as the Payor,

        promises to pay the order of:

1

1.2. _________________________________, as the Payee,
address _________________________________

1.3. the sum of $___________

2. Interest will be charged from Date at the rate of _____% per annum until paid.

3. Principal and interest will be payable in lawful money of the United States.

4. If a default occurs in payments when due, the entire sum of principal and interest will become immediately due at the option of the payee.

5. In any action to enforce this agreement, the prevailing party will receive attorney fees.

See attached Signature Page Addendum. [RPI Form 251]

Signature of Payor: ___________________________

Signature of Payor: ___________________________

The unsecured note

This is the simplest note, shown in figure 1. It is generally used to memorialize a loan, or debt, between two parties who trust each other, or should. Since there is no security, the only way to collect the obligation in default is with a lawsuit. Once a judgment has been obtained, collecting involves finding the debtor's assets, legally attaching them, then monetizing them. This is time-consuming, expensive, and often unsuccessful. Still, they can be used in real estate creative financing, and we will learn how subsequently.

Figure 2

DO NOT DESTROY THIS NOTE: When paid, this note, with Deed of Trust securing same, must be surrendered to Trustee for cancellation before reconveyance will be made

Escrow No.

STRAIGHT NOTE

$225,000.00   San Jose, California   July 22, 2022

For value received, Throckmorton and Willomena Homebuyer ("payor/trustor") promises to pay to Gotcha Savings, a California Corporation ("payee/beneficiary") or order, at place designated by ("payee/beneficiary") the principal sum of $225,000.00 dollars, with interest from September 1, 2022, until paid at the rate of 6.5% percent per annum, payable August 31, 2027.

The Deed of Trust securing this note contains the following provision: In the event the herein described property, or any part thereof, or any interest therein, is sold, agreed to be sold, conveyed, or alienated by the Trustor or by the operation of law or otherwise, all obligations secured by this instrument, irrespective of the maturity dates expressed therein, at the option of the holder hereof, and without demand or notice, shall immediately become due and payable.

Principal, interest, and all other sums which may become due in connection with this note and the deed of trust securing same, shall be payable in lawful money of the United States of America. Should default be made in any payment when due, the whole sum of principal and interest shall become immediately due at the option of the holder of this note. If action be instituted on this note, I promise to pay such sum as the Court may fix as attorney's fees.

_______________________________   _______________________________

Throckmorton Homebuyer   Willomena Homebuyer

The straight note

This note, shown in figure 2, is a loan that has one single payment at the end of its term, that is, at maturity. It can include interest, which accrues, and it can be secured to real estate by a deed of trust or mortgage, depending upon common practice in the state. These can be used for real estate, but most noteholders prefer to receive regular payments, so its use is less common. Foreclosure is the remedy in the event of a default.

Figure 3

DO NOT DESTROY THIS NOTE: When paid, this note,
with Deed of Trust securing same, must be surrendered to
Trustee for cancellation before reconveyance will be made

Escrow No.

INSTALLMENT NOTE—INTEREST INCLUDED

For value received, ("payor/trustor") promise to pay to ("payee/beneficiary") or order, at place designated by ("payee/beneficiary"), the principal sum of dollars, with interest from at the rate of percent per annum on the amounts of principal sum remaining unpaid from time to time.

Principal and interest payable in _______ installments of _______ or more each, on the _______ day of each and every _______ beginning on _______ and continuing until _______.

The Deed of Trust securing this note contains the following provision: In the event the herein described property, or any part thereof, or any interest therein, is sold, agreed to be sold, conveyed or alienated by the Trustor, or by the operation of law or otherwise, all obligations secured by this instrument, irrespective of the maturity dates expressed therein, at the option of the holder hereof, and without demand or notice, shall immediately become due and payable.

Each payment shall be credited first on interest then due and the remainder on principal; and interest shall then cease upon the principal so credited. Principal, interest, and all other sums which may become due in connection with this note and the deed of trust securing same, shall be payable in lawful money of the United States of America. Should default be made in any payment when due, the whole sum of principal and interest shall become immediately due at the option of the holder of this note. If action be instituted on this note, I promise to pay such sums as the Court may fix as attorney's fees.

_______________________________   _______________________________

The installment note—interest included

Figure 3 shows the installment note, which is written to include interest and have regular payments. Payments can be monthly, quarterly, semiannually, or annually, as the parties agree. The notes can be fully amortized, partially amortized, interest only, or even principal only. Even more creative options are possible, which will be presented later. Here, foreclosure is also the remedy in the event of a default.

Due on sale

Since about 1970, lenders have placed due on sale or transfer clauses in their notes and security instruments to prevent owners from selling or transferring to other people who have not qualified for the loan. This is named an alienation clause. When this clause is drawn into the note, as here, it is also included in the security instrument so it can be enforced. Enforcement involves the lender sending a letter to the new and former owners declaring a default, accelerating the loan (i.e., calling it immediately due and payable), and threatening foreclosure. The parties usually try to negotiate an assumption of the loan with the lender or they refinance to pay the lender off. The lender doesn't want the property, but they can and do foreclose sometimes. They don't need a carrot because they have a stick.

Security instruments

Security instruments for loans come in various types. For real estate, there are deeds of trust (figure 4) and mortgages. For furniture and the like, it's called a chattel mortgage. For motor vehicles and equipment loans, it's security agreement. All contain conditions of maintenance of the property, adherence to the terms of the note, and enforcement by foreclosure or repossession. Figure 4 is a sample deed of trust applicable in California.

Figure 4

RECORDING REQUESTED BY:

ORDER NO.:
APN:

WHEN RECORDED MAIL TO

SPACE ABOVE THIS LINE IS FOR

Deed of Trust and Assignment of Rents

This Deed of Trust, made this _________ day of _________, between _________, herein called TRUSTOR, whose address is _________, a California corporation, herein called TRUSTEE, and _________, herein called BENEFICIARY.

Bruce Kellogg

Witnesseth: That Trustor IRREVOCABLY GRANTS, TRANSFERS, AND ASSIGNS to TRUSTEE IN TRUST, WITH POWER OF SALE, that property in ___________ County, California, described as:

See "Exhibit A" attached hereto and made a part hereof.

Together with the rents, issues and profits thereof, SUBJECT, HOWEVER, to the right, power and the authority hereinafter given to and conferred upon Beneficiary to collect and apply such rents, issues and profits.

For the Purpose of Securing:

1. Performance of each agreement of Trustor herein contained. 2. Payment of the indebtedness evidenced by one promissory note of even date herewith, and extension or renewal thereof, in the principal sum of executed by Trustor in favor of Beneficiary or order. 3. Payment of such further sums as the then record owner of said property, hereafter may borrow from Beneficiary, when evidenced by another note (or notes) reciting it is so secured.

To Protect the Security of This Deed of Trust, Trustor Agrees:

(1) To keep said property in good condition and repair; not to remove or demolish any building thereon; to compete or restore promptly and in good and workmanlike manner any building which may be constructed, damaged or destroyed thereon and to pay when due all claims for labor performed and materials furnished therefor; to comply with all laws affecting said property or requiring any alterations or improvements to be made thereon; not to commit or permit waste thereof; not to commit, suffer or permit any act upon said property in violation of law; to cultivate, irrigate, fertilize, fumigate, prune and do all other acts which from the character or use of said property may be reasonably necessary, the specific enumerations herein not excluding the general.

(2) To provide, maintain and deliver to Beneficiary fire insurance satisfactory to and with loss payable to Beneficiary. The amount collected under any fire or other insurance policy may be applied by Beneficiary upon any indebtedness secured hereby and in such order as Beneficiary may determine, or at option of Beneficiary the entire amount so collected or any part thereof may be released to Trustor. Such application or release shall not cure or waive any default or notice of default hereunder or invalidate any act done pursuant to such notice.

(3) To appear in and defend any action or proceeding purporting to affect the security hereof or the rights or powers of Beneficiary or Trustee; and to pay all costs and expenses, including cost of evidence of title and attorney's fees in a reasonable sum, in any such action or proceeding in which Beneficiary or Trustee may appear, and in any suit brought by Beneficiary to foreclose this Deed.

(4) To pay: at least ten days before delinquency all taxes and assessment affecting said property, including assessment on appurtenant water stock; when due, all encumbrances, charges and liens, with interest, on said property or any part thereof, which appear to be prior or superior hereto; all costs, fees and expenses of this Trust.

Should Trustor fail to make any payment or to do any act as herein provided, then Beneficiary or Trustee, but without obligation so to do and without notice to or demand upon Trustor and without releasing Trustor from any obligation hereof, may: make or do the same in such manner and to such extent as either may deem necessary to protect the security hereof, Beneficiary or Trustee being authorized to enter upon said property for such purposes; appear in and defend any action or proceeding purporting to affect the security hereof or the rights or powers of Beneficiary or Trustee; pay, purchase, contest or compromise any encumbrance, charge or lien which in the judgment of either appears to be prior or superior hereto; and, in exercising any such powers, pay necessary expenses, employ counsel and pay his reasonable fees.

(5) To pay immediately and without demand all sums so expended by Beneficiary or Trustee, with interest from date of expenditure at the amount allowed by law in effect at the date hereof, and to pay for any statement provided for by law in effect at the date hereof regarding the obligation secured hereby any amount demanded by the Beneficiary not to exceed the maximum allowed by law at the time when said statement is demanded.

(6) That any award of damages in connection with any condemnation for public use of or injury to said property or any part thereof is hereby assigned and shall be paid to Beneficiary who may apply or release such moneys received by him in the same manner and with the same effect as above provided for disposition of proceeds of fire or other insurance.

(7) That by accepting payment of any sum secured hereby after its due date, Beneficiary does not waive his right either to require prompt payment when due of all other sums so secured or to declare default for failure so to pay.

(8) That at any time or from time to time, without liability therefor and without notice, upon written request of Beneficiary and presentation of this Deed and said note for endorsement, and without affecting the personal liability of any person for payment of the indebtedness secured hereby, Trustee may: reconvey any part of said property; consent to the making of any map or plat thereof; join in granting any easement thereon; or join in any extension agreement or any agreement subordinating the lien of charge thereof.

(9) That upon written request of Beneficiary stating that all sums secured hereby have been paid, and upon surrender of this Deed and said note to Trustee for cancellation and retention and upon payment of its fees, Trustee shall reconvey, without warranty, the property then held hereunder. The recitals in such reconveyance of any matters or facts shall be conclusive proof of the truthfulness thereof. The grantee in such reconveyance may be described as "the person or persons legally entitled thereto." Five years after issuance of such full reconveyance, Trustee may destroy said note and this Deed (unless directed in such request to retain them).

(10) That as additional security, Trustor hereby gives to and confers upon Beneficiary the right, power and authority, during the continuance of these Trusts, to collect the rents, issues and profits of said property, reserving unto Trustor the right, prior to any default by Trustor in payment of any indebtedness secured hereby or in performance of any agreement hereunder, to collect and retain such rents, issues and profits as they become due and payable. Upon any such default, Beneficiary may at any time without notice, either in person, by agent, or by a receiver to be appointed by a court, and without regard to the adequacy of any security for the indebtedness hereby secured, enter upon and take possession of said property or any part thereof, in his own name sue for or otherwise collect such rents, issues and profits, including those past due and unpaid, and apply the same, less costs and expenses of operation and collection, including reasonable attorney's fees, upon any indebtedness secured hereby, and in such order as Beneficiary may determine. The entering upon and taking possession of said property, the collection of such rents, issues and profits and the application thereof as aforesaid, shall not cure or waive any default or notice of default hereunder or invalidate any act done pursuant to such notice.

(11) That upon default by Trustor in payment of any indebtedness secured hereby or in performance of any agreement hereunder, Beneficiary may declare all sums secured hereby immediately due and payable by delivery to Trustee of written declaration of default and demand for sale and of written notice of default and of election to cause to be sold said property, which notice Trustee shall cause to be filed for record. Beneficiary also shall deposit with Trustee this Deed, said note and all documents evidencing expenditures secured hereby.

After the lapse of such time as may then be required by law following the recordation of said notice of default, and notice of sale having been given as then required by law, Trustee, without demand on Trustor, shall sell said property at the time and place fixed by it in said notice of sale, either as a whole or in separate parcels, and in such order as it may determine, at public auction to the highest bidder for cash in lawful money of the United States, payable at time of sale. Trustee may postpone sale of all or any portion of said property by public announcement at such time and place of sale, and from time to time thereafter may postpone such sale by public announcement at the time fixed by the preceding postponement. Trustee shall deliver to such purchaser its deed conveying the property so sold, but without any covenant or warranty, express or implied. The recitals in such deed of any matters or facts shall be conclusive proof of the truthfulness thereof. Any person, including Trustor, Trustee, or Beneficiary as hereinafter defined, may purchase at such sale.

After deducting all cost, fees and expenses of Trustee and of this Trust, including cost of evidence of title in connection with sale, Trustee shall apply the proceeds of sale to payment of: all sums expended under the terms hereof, not then repaid, with accrued interest at the amount allowed by law in effect at the date hereof; all other sums then secured hereby; and the remainder, if any, to the person or persons legally entitled thereto.

(12) Beneficiary, or any successor in ownership of any indebtedness secured hereby, may from time to time, by instrument in writing, substitute a successor or successors to any Trustee named herein or acting hereunder, which instrument, executed by the Beneficiary and duly acknowledged and recorded in the office of the recorder of the county or counties where said property is situated, shall be conclusive proof of proper substitution of such successor Trustee or Trustees, who shall, without conveyance from the Trustee predecessor, succeed to all its title, estate, rights, powers and duties. Said instrument must contain the name of the original Trustor, Trustee and Beneficiary hereunder, the book and page where this Deed is recorded and the name and address of the new Trustee.

(13) That this Deed applies to, inures to the benefit of, and binds all parties hereto, their heirs, legatees, devisees, administrators, executors, successors and assigns. The term Beneficiary shall mean the owner and holder, including pledges, of the note secured hereby, whether or not named as Beneficiary herein. In this Deed, whenever the context so requires, the masculine gender includes the feminine and/or neuter, and the singular number includes the plural.

(14) That Trustee accepts this Trust when this Deed, duly executed and acknowledged, is made a public record as provided by law. Trustee is not obligated to notify any party hereto of pending sale under any other Deed of Trust or of any action or proceeding in which Trustor, Beneficiary or Trustee shall be a party unless brought by Trustee.

Bruce Kellogg

The undersigned Trustor request that a copy of any Notice of Default and of any Notice of Sale hereunder be mailed to him at his address hereinbefore set forth.

_________________________________   _________________________________

A notary public or other officer completing this certificate verifies only the identity of the individual who signed the document to which this certificate is attached, and not the truthfulness, accuracy, or validity of that document.

State of _________________________________

County of _________________________________

On _________________________ before me, _________________________ a Notary Public, personally appeared ____, who proved to me on the basis of satisfactory evidence to be the person(s) whose name(s) is/are subscribed to the within instrument and acknowledged to me that he/she/they executed the same in his/her/their authorized capacity(ies), and that by his/her/their signature(s) on the instrument the person(s), or the entity upon behalf of which the person(s) acted, executed the instrument.

I certify under PENALTY OF PERURY under the laws of the State of California that the foregoing paragraph is true and correct.

WITNESS my hand and official seal.

Signature: _________________________________

Name: _________________________________
       (Typed or Printed)   (Seal)

Chapter 2

Purchase and Sale Agreements

Types of agreements

Purchase and sale agreements are used for all real estate trans-actions due, among other things, to the Statute of Frauds, which requires all real estate agreements to be in writing in order to be enforceable. This includes modifications such as amendments, extensions, and cancellations.

These agreements come in all shapes and sizes. At the lower end are the one- or two-page versions taught by trainers, coaches, and "gurus." These are kept simple on purpose so as not to be confusing to sellers at kitchen table negotiations.

In the middle, and most common, are agreements used by the real estate brokerage industry. These run eight to fifteen pages, not including addenda for disclosure and special purposes. They are extensive because they need to minimize legal liabilities for all involved, including buyers, sellers, and their brokerage representatives. Since most brokers and agents are not legally trained, the agreements are prepared for them to mostly fill in the blanks.

At the high end are agreements drawn by law firms. This is more common in commercial and larger transactions. We won't be working with those here.

Our approach

In this book, we will be using the agreement in appendix A. It is legally sound and evenhanded to be fair to both buyers and sellers. Since our topic here is creative financing, we will be dealing with the

11

financial terms of the transaction, and only incidentally addressing other terms in the agreement. Appendix B contains optional attachments that might apply and be chosen to augment the agreement itself.

Customization

The creative financing included here is applicable to any agreement discussed above. Just include it in whatever agreement that has been chosen to be used. Legal review would be a good idea to make sure it has been done properly.

An educational resource

Many state and local real estate broker associations offer courses on contracts to their members. Some of these accept the public into the courses for a modest fee. Serious investors who intend to scale their business should take advantage of this. You can't know too much about what you are signing!

Chapter 3

Seller Financing

In a real estate transaction, seller financing takes place when the seller and the buyer agree that the seller will lend some of the purchase price to the buyer to facilitate the sale. This is often labelled owner will carry (OWC) and is a well-trodden path in residential, commercial, and land transactions.

How is it done?

As in any real estate transaction, the buyer and the seller negotiate the terms of the loan, including the amount, due date, interest rate, and monthly payment. Other terms could include a late charge and a due-on-sale clause and more.

The documents consist of a promissory note and a deed of trust or mortgage, depending upon the laws of the state for securing loans to real property. Depending upon the state, an attorney, escrow company, or title company will prepare the documents for the parties, making the process very straightforward, though not necessarily simple.

Negotiating the terms

Down payments are usually between 10 percent and 30 percent, depending upon the buyer's financial position, the buyer's creditworthiness, and the seller's need for cash. A credit report on the buyer is essential.

It is possible to have a loan where the payments are interest only, but some degree of amortization is preferable so the buyer is building up equity and can refinance more readily in the future. The interest rate should be a market rate, or less if lending to a friend or family member. Excessive interest rates do nobody any good, just making it harder for the buyer to succeed with the property.

The length (term) of the loan is negotiable based on the needs of the parties. The note could be written with one or more options to extend in case conditions for refinancing are not favorable when the loan matures. The idea is not to create a condition where the buyer cannot pay off the loan when it comes due.

What about collecting payments and property taxes?

Sometimes with seller financing, the buyer will neglect to pay the property taxes or keep the premises insured. The best way to prevent this is to hire a loan servicing company. They will do everything, and even foreclose, if the need arises. The cost is reasonable, and the piece of mind is priceless! Who pays is negotiable.

What if the buyer defaults?

There are three alternatives. The obvious one is to hire an attorney or foreclosure company to legally recover the property. Then, it'll be necessary to make repairs and resell the property or rent it out. This should be chosen if the buyer's default appears to be permanent and cannot be corrected.

If the buyer's default appears to be temporary, a job loss, for example, then it's best to suspend payments. Once the situation is resolved, modify the note to include the missed payments and proceed as before.

The third alternative is to sell the note at a discount and let someone else deal with the default. Discounts on defaulted notes are typically 40–80 percent. This is a terrible idea. Try to avoid doing it.

What if the seller needs money later?

There are several alternatives here also. The first is to sell the entire note at a discount. Since the note will be performing (i.e., not in default), the discount could be in the 20–30 percent range, which isn't so bad if you need the cash.

But maybe you don't need to sell the entire note. You could sell just part of the note or just a certain number of the payments. There are markets for notes across the country and over the Internet. Notes can be very liquid nowadays!

Finally, you could borrow against the note. The legal term for this is hypothecation. Private parties, banks, credit unions, and factoring companies all do note hypothecations. Check the Internet first.

Benefits to the buyer

There are two primary benefits to the buyer. The first is that the buyer can negotiate a customized loan with the seller to accommodate the buyer's circumstances. Banks and mortgage brokers usually sell their loans on Wall Street, so the loans are standardized. These don't necessarily fit everyone.

In addition, commercial lenders charge loan origination fees, also known as points. Most sellers do not charge fees for lending, and in many states they cannot. This saves quite a bit for the buyer.

Benefits to the seller

There are two benefits to the seller also. The first is that carrying some financing facilitates the sale. No doubt about it!

Secondly, the note that is carried back generates a regular monthly income stream that is secured directly by the property with which the seller is very familiar. This makes it a very good, long-term investment for them.

Chapter 4

Seller-Carryback Note Terms

Introduction

It is well known among real estate investors that some of the best deals occur when the seller is persuaded to carry some or all the financing. This topic provides a menu of terms that can be negotiated into the note. So far as drawing up the note is concerned, most closing agents (i.e., escrow officers and attorneys) have what is called a cookbook of legally correct note terms, so buyers and sellers need not be concerned about such details.

The note terms negotiated for the transaction are specified in the financing section of the purchase and sale agreement. Chapter 2 refers to appendix A for this. Additionally, the remainder of this chapter presents the most common note terms used in seller-carryback financing. There are others, of course, but they are less common. An experienced real estate agent, broker, or attorney should be able to help identify any that are unique to the contemplated transaction.

1) *Request for notice of delinquency.* This is actually not a term in the note. It is prepared in escrow and recorded instead. Its purpose is for the senior lienholder(s) to notify the carryback seller in the event the owner is not paying them. It protects the seller by allowing them to jump in early to protect their note.

2) *Unsecured.* This also is not a term of the note. It should be inserted at the top of the note to indicate that there is no security instrument (i.e., mortgage or deed of trust) secur-

ing the note to the property. It is not recommended, however, because the buyer could further encumber the property, or even sell it, without the noteholder finding out.

3) *Late charge.* Most notes have a late charge, such as 3 percent of the payment after ten days past due. Some states have regulations for owner-occupied properties. Most investment transactions are not regulated in this way. Check what is legal in your state. Some court cases have resulted in all interest being refunded!

4) *Due on sale or transfer.* This term is included to protect the seller from the property being resold or transferred to a party other than the original buyer. After all, the secondary buyer might not be creditworthy. However, in order to be enforceable, this term must also be included in the security instrument (mortgage or deed of trust). The text in the note and in the security instrument should be identical, word for word, for successful enforcement. Other note terms do not need to be included in the security instrument, but this one does.

5) *Assumption.* If the parties desire for the note to be assumable, this can be included in the note. Usually, some criteria are included to protect the seller. Often the note says that the seller's approval "cannot be unreasonably withheld" when there are protections included. A simple text could be as follows: The obligation for the repayment of this note can be assumed by another party at any time in the future, retaining the same terms and conditions.

   The other thing to know is if assumption is not mentioned in the note, then the note is legally assumable. Seller permission is not needed.

6) *Balloon payment.* When a note is not fully amortized such that a balance remains at maturity, this is called a balloon payment. If this applies, the note should be written to clearly include this feature to protect both parties from misunderstanding.

7) *Option to extend.* If a balloon payment is involved, writing an option to extend into a note could prevent a rough ending if refinancing or selling conditions are unfavorable. It could extend for a year or two with a fee paid to the seller or a partial paydown made.

   A simple text could be as follows: "At maturity, and at the buyer's option, this note can be extended for an additional X number of years at Y percent interest."

   Options are as follows: a) raise the interest rate, b) raise the payment, c) make a partial paydown of principal, or interest being carried, if any.

8) *Interest only.* Describes the arrangement where the payments consist only of interest and a balloon payment occurs at maturity.

9) *Zero interest.* Involves payments of principal only with no interest being charged. This term is a sweetie for buyers!

10) *Deferred interest.* Involves interest accruing to maturity, when both principal and interest are due. Although this helps cash flow, unlike zero interest, it is very risky. Rapid appreciation will be essential for this to succeed, and losing the property is a realistic possibility.

11) *Skip a payment.* Sometimes, if the parties are relating well, it is possible to include a term allowing the borrower to skip a payment in the event of job loss, rental vacancy, or other misfortune. This can be made part of the note or dealt with at the time. Including it ahead of time is preferable for a more stable transaction.

12) *Substitution of collateral.* Sometimes an enterprising buyer will negotiate with the seller the right to move the note and secure it to a different property. This is usually done to sell, exchange, or refinance the property. There should be criteria stated in the note to protect the noteholder, but approval "should not be unreasonably withheld if the criteria are met.

   An example term wording could be as follows: "Seller agrees to a future substitution of the collateral securing this note, provided that the new collateral has equal or greater equity."

13) *Right of first refusal.* Sometimes an enterprising buyer will realize that the seller might decide to sell the note at a discount to raise cash in the future. Including this term gives the buyer first shot at buying their own debt back at a discount, effectively lowering the purchase price. An example wording could be as follows: "At any time in the future, should the seller decide to sell this note to a third party, the buyer reserves the right to redeem this note for the amount the seller would have accepted from the third party."

14) *No prepayment penalty.* Legally-speaking, if a term is not included in a note, it is considered not to apply. It might be wise not to include this term. Here is a text if the decision is to include it: "Borrower retains the right to pay any portion of this note, or any accumulated interest, at any time prior to maturity without any penalty."

15) *Prepayment discount.* "Seller agrees to discount this note by X percent should buyer fully prepay principal and accrued interest at any time prior to the due date in the first Y years."

16) *Subordination.* Sometimes a buyer will want to refinance with a new first loan yet still replace the seller's carryback loan back on the property, possibly paying down some of it. This involves a subordination, where the seller's loan is lifted from the title, then put back down after the new first loan has been obtained.

Here is a text for that: "Seller agrees to subordinate this note and its deed of trust to any new financing by any buyer at any time in the future, provided that the total encumbrances will not exceed X percent of an appraised value of the property." Order an appraisal to avoid a dispute.

17) *Graduated Payment Mortgage (GPM).* This is a note designed such that interest and/or payments start low then increase gradually over the years. It makes for easier ownership but can become a trap in the later years. For this reason, the Dodd-Frank legislation prohibits this type of

loan on 1–4 unit owner-occupied properties, but it is still legal for investment property transactions of all kinds. A competent agent, broker, or real estate attorney should be able to design a GPM for an investment transaction.

18) *Shared Appreciation Mortgage (SAM)*. This is a popular note term when prices are high and still rapidly rising or when interest rates are high. The note is written so that the seller receives payments that are submarket but also receives a percentage of the property's appreciation upon sale or maturation of the note. It is useful, but not very common. A note text for a SAM could be as follows: "When this property is being sold, seller will receive payoff of their note plus X % of the net sale proceeds." (See chapter 6 for more detail.)

Conclusion

Clearly, these note terms are not appropriate for every transaction. Sellers would not agree to all of them either. Buyers should select a few that are particularly important to them and negotiate as many as they can. Remember, too, that you can give some on price in order to get advantageous terms.

Chapter 5

Using Notes to Buy and Sell

Notes are an alternative to cash

Real estate is commonly bought and sold using cash for a down payment or for the full purchase price. People rarely think of using something else. This topic presents ten ways of using notes in real estate transactions.

A primer on notes

It's really simple. A note is a unilateral contract promising to repay a loan under certain terms and conditions. Notes can be unsecured, or they can be enforced using a security instrument such as a mortgage, deed of trust, chattel mortgage, or a security agreement.

About priority

The order in which documents are recorded or registered (same thing) at the county is called priority. Regarding notes, if a mortgage is recorded on a free-and-clear property on a Tuesday, it is in first position. Another one recorded on Thursday would be a second mortgage. When one is paid off, those remaining all move up one position in priority. This should help in understanding the discussion that follows.

No. 1: Making yourself a loan!

In 1980, I owned seven rental houses. A realtor brought me a thirty-unit, off-market apartment opportunity. The agent taught me how to write seven notes secured by deeds of trust to use as the down payment for an institutional first loan on the apartments rather than coming up with the cash. The seller accepted the notes, and I was introduced to creative financing using notes. Zoom! We're off!

Can this be done today? No and yes. It will not work with major lenders who package their loans into securities then sell them on Wall Street to replenish their supply of lendable funds. It will work with portfolio lenders who retain the loans that they make. This includes local banks, credit unions, and private lenders.

No. 2: A note then a "subject to"

This method is easier to explain and do. When you find a seller who will allow you to take title subject to their existing loan, write them a note and give it to them as part or all of your down payment. If they will accept your 1984 Mercedes or your bass boat, so much the better! Conserve your cash if you can!

No. 3: Prepaying interest with a note

Suppose you owe a note secured by real estate, and the property is experiencing a negative cash flow. The note was carried back by the seller, and they have an ample other income. You can improve your cash flow by creating a new note secured by another property that pays for one year's interest on the seller's note and give it to the seller. A financially comfortable seller will likely take it. The terms would be negotiable.

No. 4: All-inclusive deed of trust (mortgage)

Suppose you meet a seller who has a first loan at a low interest rate, and you want to take title subject to that obligation, and the seller will carry back a note as well.

You can create a new note that wraps the first loan and the seller's portion at a higher interest rate than the first loan so the seller receives a high blended interest rate. This can be enticing for some sellers due to the higher yield they will receive. You can also use this method when you are the seller.

No. 5: Graduated payment mortgage (GPM)

Suppose you are selling a property, and under the terms, the buyer will experience a negative cash flow. You can create a carryback loan that starts with a submarket interest rate and graduates annually up to market rate, or even a bit above. You do the same with the payments such that your buyer's payments are not, or less, negative. When buying, you can do the same. Be aware that Dodd-Frank prohibits institutional lenders from making GPM loans on one to four residential, owner-occupied units, but this is private lending taking place here, so it's okay.

No. 6: Shared appreciation mortgage (SAM)

In some areas, there is historically high appreciation, but cash flow is weak, tending to be negative. The Bay Area is a good example. If the seller is in a position to carry back a first loan, then create a shared appreciation mortgage (SAM), where the seller receives a percentage of the appreciation at the time of the sale in return for accepting a submarket interest rate and payments on their note.

No. 7: Splitting notes

Notes can be split up. For example, suppose you are buying a property where the seller will carry back a first loan. They are older, and they are planning their estate. If they have several heirs, the carryback loan can be divided into separate notes intended for each heir. They need not be equal in amount, and they can be secured by one mortgage or deed of trust.

No. 8: Allocating interest between notes

Sometimes a seller will be agreeable to carrying back a note, but they might ask, "What if I need money later on?" The answer is to create a senior note and load most or all of the interest and payments onto it. This note is designed to be sold, but at a low discount if the seller needs money. The junior note is meant to be held by the seller until the balloon payoff since it is not desirable for a discounted sale. There is also the possibility of creating multiple senior notes so they can be peeled off and sold individually as needed.

No. 9: Family note financing

Nowadays, young people have trouble buying a home while their parents often have substantial pension fund assets and/or real estate equity. In this case, parents can help by participating in the home purchase, where their children sign multiple notes back to their parents for the funds that the parents contributed. These notes can be sized to be forgiven annually under the federal Gift Act. This is a good estate distribution technique for the parents and a home-buying assist for the children.

No. 10: Zero down technique

Once in a while, you could come across a seller who will let you take title subject to their first loan and create a junior/second loan that can be sold at a discount to give the seller a cash down payment. This requires the property to have a built-in discount for someone to be willing to buy the note. As in no. 8 above, interest can be loaded onto this note so that the discount is not too great. A third loan with no interest or payments can be created for any of the seller's equity that remains.

Wrapping up

This discussion is not meant to be exhaustive of all the possibilities of using notes to buy and sell real estate. It is introductory, intended to open the reader's mind to the use of notes.

Chapter 6

Shared Appreciation Mortgage

What is it?

A shared appreciation mortgage (SAM) is a mortgage carried back by a seller in which the seller shares in the appreciation of the property when a sale, refinance, or the loan termination occurs. A SAM is a seller-carryback loan that is not to be confused with institutional investors sharing appreciation with homeowners, which came about these past few years as prices rocketed.

Applications

When the market is appreciating rapidly, it is sometimes difficult to convince a seller to sell on reasonable terms or to carry back owner financing. The SAM involves a low interest rate but then gives the seller a percentage of the profit at the end of the loan term. This approach also works in a high-interest-rate environment because it helps the buyer to achieve a reasonable cash flow to sustain the property.

A standard form for this kind of note can sometimes be found on the Internet since it is simply a promissory note with a few custom terms added. A real estate attorney or escrow officer can probably accomplish this.

Benefits for the Seller

1) Use of a SAM gets the property sold, often at full price.
2) Installment sale under IRC 453 can defer income taxes.

3) Seller doesn't have to make payments on senior loans anymore.
4) Eases a sale when prices are high.
5) Eases a sale when interest rates are high.
6) Seller can trade the note, sell all or part of it, or borrow against it (i.e., hypothecate/collateralize it.)

It is important to deal with intelligent, good-natured sellers. The relationship will require maintenance. Additionally, the seller must believe that the property will appreciate over the term of the loan or they will not accept the SAM. Finally, do expect the seller to take the proposal to an attorney. For best success, arm them for the meeting, or even arrange to go with them.

Benefits for the Buyer

1) Good for buying in high-priced markets and/or high interest rates.
2) Price is less important than usual.
3) Terms are negotiable, building a relationship with the seller.
4) SAM facilitates the purchase.

Some investors in high-priced areas just don't want to buy out of area for all kinds of reasons. They prefer to keep their money close by. Using a SAM can make this possible. The same is true if interest rates are rising or are high. A SAM can be used to still make acquisitions.

The best opportunities are the ones where the seller has substantial equity. The more there is, the more payments can be reduced by the seller participating. It depends whether first and/or second loans exist how much seller participation can be. Ideally, the SAM should be structured to give the buyer a positive cash flow, at least. There are always risks such as a vacancy, eviction, rehab, damaging events (e.g., fire, wind, flooding). Clearly, breakeven won't be enough.

Considerations

Sometimes a seller might not be enthusiastic about carrying back a SAM but does want to accomplish their sale. In this instance, to encourage the buyer to pay off early (by selling or refinancing), the parties could include a phase-out clause that reduces the seller's percentage based on an earlier payoff.

Another consideration is that a SAM works well for property flippers, particularly in a rising market. Typically, the term is under a year because that is often the time frame for a rehab and sale. The flipper gets lower interest costs, and the seller gets a share of the profit. This is a good way to convince the seller to make the deal.

Also, when selling a property, a SAM can be carried back for the benefits listed above. This is especially true of the installment sale under section 453 of the Internal Revenue Code. The net profit is basically spread out over the term of the loan, which could reduce the applicable tax bracket. For the seller, it's the longer, the better. Definitely consult a tax professional when taking advantage of this.

Chapter 7

Land Sale Contract

What is it?

A land sale contract is a version of the purchase and sale agreement commonly used in real estate transactions with some important departures. It has been around a long time, probably over a hundred years, but it received increased use in the 1970s when institutional lenders began including due-on-sale clauses in their notes and security instruments (i.e., deed of trust or mortgage).

This resulted in the Garn-St. Germain Act of 1982 (12 U.S. Code 1701j-3-Preemption of Due-on-Sale Prohibitions). Under the definitions, it says, "(1) the 'due-on-sale' clause means a contract provision which authorizes a lender, at its option, to declare due and payable sums secured by the lender's security instrument if all or any part of the property, or an interest therein, securing the real property loan is sold or transferred without the lender's prior written consent."

The land sale contract has important uses and benefits, which are discussed below.

Characteristics

Under the land sale contract, the seller, called vendor, retains title to the property, while the buyer, called vendee, receives possession and makes payments to the vendor until the vendor is fully paid. The contract is usually not processed through an escrow, recorded at the county, or the receipt of title insurance. It is purposely off the record. Nobody—competitors, investigators, family and exes, creditors, lenders—are supposed to know of the new ownership. In this case, there are no closing costs either.

The Internal Revenue Service considers it a sale when the vendor receives money from the vendee and delivers possession to them. For the vendor, the sale could be set up as an installment sale under IRC 453(b)(1) to defer taxes on capital gains over the term of the contract. Professional tax advice for this should be sought, along with tax effects at the state level.

Property taxes, on the other hand, are not reassessed upon the sale because the tax assessor is not made aware of the sale by recordation of a deed. Down the road, when a deed is finally recorded, all the escaped taxes plus penalties and costs fall due. This could hit some buyer down the ownership chain who gets stuck with all the back taxes. The county has seen this before!

The land sale contract is actually a mortgage in effect because fee ownership via a deed is not given to the vendee until all sums are paid. Moreover, it is a nonrecourse purchase money transaction. The vendee cannot be held responsible for any loss the vendor incurs in the event the vendee defaults.

Land sale contracts come both with and without power of sale provisions. Those without do not give the vendee a path to reinstate in the event of a default. With the power of sale, the vendee can reinstate. Both versions can be foreclosed by a judicial foreclosure, but then the vendee has the right of redemption to recover the property by paying the principal balance, back interest, and all costs. The duration of this right varies by state, but since the vendee has an equitable interest in the property, they have the right to recover if they can.

Disclosure responsibilities

In California, if a licensed real estate agent or broker is involved in a land sale contract transaction, they are required to provide the vendee with disclosures regarding the use of the land sale contract, and disclosures of the condition of the property. Private parties do not have these disclosure requirements, although making such disclosures is a good idea to avoid disputes. Users of the land sale contract should learn the rules applicable in their state.

Applications/benefits

The land sale contract is mostly applied in three instances:

1) when a lender's due-on-sale clause is being avoided,
2) when a buyer is not lender-qualified, but is trusted enough to enter the transaction; and
3) when public notice of the transaction is not desired.

Disadvantages

Disadvantages arise due to the fact that the ownership is retained by the vendor and not transferred by a deed at the time the contract is fully executed. The vendor could overencumber the property or even sell it without the vendee even knowing. This would create a big mess. If the vendor borrows against the property up to the purchase price with the vendee, that is permissible. They are just extracting their equity and can still fulfill their contract with the vendee. Besides that, if the vendor sells the property, they have defrauded the vendee.

Buyer's default and foreclosure

Under a land sale contract, the vendee is required to make payments to the vendor, pay the property taxes, and keep the property insured, with the vendor included on the policy. Failure to do any of these is a default on the contract and is eligible for foreclosure by the vendor. Since it is a contract, foreclosure would be judicial (i.e., through the courts), which is time-consuming and expensive. This is why a power of sale should be included in the contract to speed up the foreclosure. Even so, the vendee still has the right of redemption provided by state law.

Contract termination

Besides judicial foreclosure, or under a power of sale provision, the alternative contract termination is a quitclaim deed from the vendee to the vendor. Some vendors obtain this up front and keep it ready to record if the vendee defaults. Other times, if the vendee is not in default, it can be recorded with the vendee's permission. There are two problems here. First, the land sale contract is unrecorded, so a title insurer will be confused by finding a recorded quitclaim. Second, the vendee has an equitable interest, so what to do with that?

The best solution is for the vendor and vendees to go to a title company and discuss the best way to obtain an insurable title for the vendor. With the unrecorded contract, equitable interest, and right of redemption all hanging out there, this is no time to do it yourself on the cheap. The vendor just might have to compensate the vendee for some of their equity and pay some transfer expenses to restore a clean title. Or a quiet title court action might be necessary. Whew!

Alternatives

No financing method is ideal, even cash. They all have disadvantages of some sort. The land sale contract is complicated because the vendor retains fee simple title yet the vendee enjoys an equitable interest. There are two alternatives, as follows:

1) *Lease option.* Here the buyer leases and gets possession, but does not get an equitable interest. They can purchase by exercising their option at any time before its expiration.
2) *All-inclusive deed of trust.* Here the buyer gets the deed and possession and just owes the seller note payments. No muss, no fuss.

For readers who want to obtain a pdf for a land sale contract, these can readily be found on the Internet.

Chapter 8

Equity Sharing

What is it?

There are two kinds of shared equity models out there lately. We will discuss both of them in turn.

No. 1. The first can be called an equity sharing company because it is an institutional investor. Homebuyers and homeowners have four options for raising cash: a) home equity loans, b) cash-out refinancing, c) home equity lines of credit (HELOC), or d) home equity sharing.

The last choice is different. The institutional investor obtains an appraisal on the property then offers up to 20 percent cash for part ownership in the home. It is not a loan, so there is no interest and there are no payments. When the home sells, or is refinanced, the investor is paid their part of the appreciation plus their initial investment.

Here are five companies with location and year that they were founded.

1)   Unison, San Francisco, 2013
2)   EquiFi, San Jose, 2015
3)   Hometap, Boston, 2019
4)   Point, Palo Alto, 2015
5)   Unlock, San Jose, year not found

Pros and cons

This form of equity sharing is not a debt for the homeowner, and some of these companies will invest even if the homeowners have credit scores as low as 500. The company simply adjusts the amount they offer to compensate for lower credit scores.

Negatives of this model are that they are available up to twenty states, depending on the company, but not in every state. In addition, only principal single-family residences are eligible.

Potential problem

There could be a problem developing with this business model, however. Note that all these companies originated after 2012, when the Great Recession began recovering with extensive Federal Reserve Bank monetary stimulus. Home prices boomed for ten years. These companies designed their business models to prosper in an appreciating market. Prices are declining 10–20–30 percent across the country now, however, with no end in sight.

I believe that these institutions will not last in their present form. So we will move on to the second shared equity model that has lasted more than forty-five years. It can be used by investors and homebuyers today.

Second model

No. 2. Equity sharing is where a private investor and a potential homeowner buy a single-family residence together and the aspiring homeowner occupies it. They can be called the resident co-owner (RCO), and the investor is called the investor co-owner (ICO). Percentage shares are negotiable, with the RCO paying the property taxes, insurance, loan payments, and routine repairs, while the ICO puts up the down payment and closing costs. There is a shared equity agreement or joint ownership agreement, which sets the term, allocates the income tax benefits, discusses possible events like divorce, and specifies how the venture is to be wound up.

Resident co-owner (RCO) benefits are as follows:

a) Home ownership now
b) No down payment or closing costs
c) No landlord and rent receipts
d) Appreciation potential
e) Income tax benefits
f) Inflation hedge

Investor co-owner (ICO) benefits are as follows:

a) Low-risk investment
b) High return potential
c) No negative cash flow
d) One-time investment
e) Income tax benefits
f) Inflation hedge
g) No management or maintenance problems

Applications

Here are three applications of equity sharing to show how it can be used.

1) As a realtor, I represented a Lockheed engineer who was a bachelor. He used his pension account to set up seven equity shares for his young relatives to achieve home ownership while growing his retirement fund.

2) I also represented a psychiatrist who purchased a house near the college where his nephew was a student. The nephew rented out bedrooms to other students. They had an equity share. After the nephew graduated, they sold the house. The nephew got married and used his share to buy a home for his wife and future family.

3) My broker (at the time) and an attorney made a business of equity sharing. They formed limited partnerships to raise

money then create equity shares with investors and home-buyers. They wrote articles and gave public and industry seminars. Altogether, they did about three hundred equity shares. They earned an organization fee and a management fee, and the broker earned real estate commissions. It was a profitable venture helping future homeowners get started.

Winding up

Equity sharing arrangements typically wind up by selling the property or one party buying out the other. Either party can buy out the other based on an appraisal. Usually, the RCO cashes out, often to acquire a whole property rather than share next time. The ICO, being an investor, will cash out and pay taxes on their gain or conduct an IRC 1031 tax-deferred exchange into another investment property to save taxes. Both parties come out ahead in their chosen direction.

Risks and precautions

The only risk area is the resident co-owner (RCO) defaulting by not paying their obligations, maintaining the property, dying, getting divorced, or filing bankruptcy. These are covered in the equity-sharing agreement, but an attorney will be needed to deal with them.

If the parties are intelligent, good-natured, and made fully informed, all usually goes well. The agreement is complicated, exceeding twenty pages, including addenda. Meeting with a knowledgeable attorney for explanations is essential.

Additionally, when buying the property, it is important for the parties to receive the set of disclosures that brokers or agents usually provide. Obtain physical inspections such as pest control, roof, and property inspection. If a broker or agent is not involved, it would be wise to hire one for an hourly fee to process the disclosures and arrange for inspections. The parties can split the cost.

Resources

There are over ten books on equity sharing on the Internet presently. Look on eBay, Amazon, and Barnes & Noble. Buy several, used, and cheap.

Also, equity-sharing agreements are available on the Internet. You can have your attorney customize one cheaply for your transaction by downloading one initially for them to use.

Chapter 9

Leases and Options

A timely subject

From 1980 to 2020, mortgage rates dropped from a peak of about 18 percent to a low of about 3 percent due to monetary and fiscal actions by the federal government. This is reversing somewhat, and among other consequences, leases and options are gathering investor interest. National trainers and coaches are bringing out courses in response.

So this chapter is descriptive of these subjects rather than instructive. The many books do that. This is introductory, emphasizing applications. Purchase some books if you want to get involved.

Option to purchase

An option confers the right, but not the obligation, to do something. Real estate examples include the option to purchase, option to lease, option to renew, option to extend, and so on. Usually, a prospective buyer negotiates an option to purchase when they want to purchase, but sometime later. They give the owner some option consideration for the right to purchase the property on mutually agreed terms on or before a specified future date. Option consideration is frequently cash, but it could be personal property, like a used tractor, or even personal service, where the future buyer fixes up the property before buying it. If the option is not exercised, the owner is entitled to keep the consideration. A good practice is to obtain a quitclaim deed and record it if the option is not exercised. This cleans up the title.

Options are particularly useful for reserving properties without appearing on the public record until the options are exercised. Developers do this to accumulate parcels without tipping off other players in the market that they are buying. An individual can negotiate an option in an appreciating market and exercise the option later without the costs of ownership in the meantime. It's an excellent way to speculate, and fortunes can be made this way.

Lease option

A lease option involves leasing and taking possession of the property being optioned. Prior to exercising the option, the property can be occupied as a residence or leased to a subtenant. This is a way to tie up a property to take advantage of an appreciating market.

Another possibility is to enter into a contract of sale with an owner, then lease option the property to a tenant. If/when the tenant exercises the option, they pay off the contract of sale, and you realize the profit. Option consideration from the tenant can be used for the down payment on the contract of sale, resulting in a (nearly) cashless transaction. This can be done repeatedly as a business model.

Two cautionary remarks are the following: a) Always make sure the option and lease agreements are separate documents so a judge cannot order the refund of the option consideration to the tenant by characterizing it as a rental deposit. Using different dates for the documents helps too. b) Obtain a quitclaim deed any time the option is not exercised in order to maintain a clean title.

Master lease option

This method applies primarily to commercial rehabilitation projects, including apartment properties. The idea is to find a building that has gotten away from its owner and become run-down with vacancies that are not being filled. A master lease is negotiated with the owner to take over rehabbing and retenanting the building, along with an option to purchase before an agreed future date when financing the purchase is more likely to succeed. Since the present owner is obviously short of funds, the purchaser will have to fund the project and receive a lower price or credit toward the purchase or both. It is best to have a real estate attorney draw up these agreements.

Moving forward

Coaches are teaching that lease options are good for three or four paydays, as follows: 1) the initial option consideration, 2) the monthly cash flow, 3) the loan principal paydown, and 4) the profit upon the sale. Several coaches have expensive programs. One is one hundred thousand dollars at the top level. Another is sixty thousand dollars, but they say they do it all for you. Then there's one that turns it into a partnership where you find the deal, they provide some funds, and they get half of your deal. I suggest purchasing a few books, get familiar, then pursue coaching if you want. Insist on value for your tuition.

Chapter 10

Necessary Disclosures

Why disclose?

Since the subject here is real estate financing, disclosure is needed in many cases. Simply put, it protects everybody from losses and other unintended consequences.

Real Estate Settlement Procedures Act (1974)

The first major real estate loan disclosure law is the Real Estate Settlement Procedures Act of 1974 (RESPA), *et seq.*, which is intended to "protect homeowners by assisting them in becoming better educated while shopping for real estate services, and eliminating kickbacks and referral fees" (Wikipedia). It applies to owner-occupant buyers of one to four residential properties and affects lenders, loan brokers, and loan servicers. This can fall under creative financing if the buyer is going to live in the property and a loan broker is arranging a loan on the property, even if the seller is carrying additional financing, say, a second loan.

Dodd-Frank Wall Street Reform and Consumer Protection Act (2010)

This act also applies to any seller-carryback transaction where the purchaser will occupy one unit as their principal residence. Additionally, a seller can do only three such transactions per year, or else they will be considered a mortgage broker and be subject to related requirements.

The law specifies certain loan terms that are to be included or excluded. A prudent investor who uses creative financing would be best advised to hire a licensed loan broker to complete the financing aspect of the transaction and split the cost or something.

What else?

From the above, the reader will notice that only owner-occupant buyers of one to four units are involved. So land, commercial, and five-plus apartment deals do not require formal financing disclosures. This does not mean that none should be made, however. At the least, the seller/lender should be given a credit report on the buyer and, ideally, a financial statement as well. Stamp both as read and approved, have all parties sign, give everyone a copy, and put them in the file. That protects everyone.

Chapter 11

Dealing with Negative Cash Flow

The problem for investors

As property prices rise in many markets across the country, it is becoming increasingly difficult for investors to acquire properties with a positive cash flow. Nowadays, it is all the more important to know how to deal with negative cash flow (NCF). Here are a number of solutions.

Intelligent property selection

Although it should be obvious, the first step to avoiding NCF is to resolve to acquire only properties that don't have it or can be structured not to have it. Especially in strong markets, some investors adopt the position that NCF doesn't matter because the market will bail them out through appreciation or rising rents. This doesn't always happen. Buy intelligently in the first place!

Increase the units

It's pretty well known in real estate investing that the more units acquired, the greater the cash flow for any given price range. For example, in Silicon Valley, a 7-plex for $1.4 million will probably cash flow better than a $1.2 million four-plex. Generally speaking for more cash flow, buy as many units as possible.

Buy better quality

It is also well known that low-income properties suffer from greater turnover, more vacancies, and higher maintenance expenses. They are also more management intensive. Buy better quality whenever possible. Leave the war zone properties to the commandos!

Transaction structuring

After a qualifying property is identified, structure the transaction for success. This involves the right price, the right down payment, the right entity (e.g., partnership), the right loan terms, and so on. Over the long term, proper design of the transaction is probably the most important step.

Lower the price

Although intuitive, the first step toward reducing NCF is to negotiate a lower price. Go back and forth several times if necessary. It will benefit throughout the entire ownership period.

Set up a cash reserve

When structuring the purchase, if there will be an unavoidable NCF, set up a cash reserve for the period that cash flow is projected to be negative. It could be a cash account, or a tax refund, or a note payoff, pending inheritance, whatever. But get it done!

Offsets

Another approach is to designate a specific note or specific property in the portfolio that has a sufficient positive cash flow to serve as an offset to the NCF. But be sure to tie the two together. Don't just say, "The portfolio can cover it." Often, that kind of loose thinking can get an investor overextended as more properties are acquired.

Recruit partners

Usually, an effective way to handle NCF is through the use of a partner. There are several kinds of these. An investor/partner could be brought in with a limited partnership (LP) or a tenancy in common (TIC). Or in some instances, it is possible to partner with the seller using a lease option or a shared appreciation mortgage (SAM). It is also possible to partner with a tenant using a lease option (rent to own) or equity sharing. These all work well under the right circumstances. Other chapters in this book cover these.

Creative carryback financing

If there is seller financing in the transaction, there are several note terms that will reduce NCF. One is to delay the first payment as long as the seller will agree, perhaps a year. Another is to agree to interest-only or principal-only payments. How about accruing all payments until maturity? (That's a risky one!) And on commercial property transactions, the graduated payment mortgage (GPM) is still possible under Dodd-Frank.

Improve operations

Many times when an investor purchases a property, it is with the objective of enhancing its performance. This typically involves raising rents, reducing expenses, increasing occupancy, and improving management. All these actions will reduce NCF.

Airbnb

A new investment type, Airbnb, has come on the scene and generally offers impressively strong cash flows. This is outside the scope of this book, but the reader is advised to investigate it to see if it is for them. Start with an Internet search.

Conclusion

Even in highly appreciated markets, it is still possible to invest and deal with NCF. You just have to learn how or work with an expert who knows. Because market conditions change, it is prudent to factor a possible 10–15 percent rent decrease or vacancy factor increase into the calculations. You don't want to get caught short at an inopportune time. Having an unused credit line is also a good idea.

Chapter 12

Dealing with Balloon Payments

Amortizing versus Balloon notes

An amortizing note is one where the principal amount is paid off over the term of the loan. A balloon note is one where the payments are not sufficient to retire the debt, and an outstanding balance is due at maturity.

What is the problem?

The problem arises when the borrower does not have the funds necessary to pay the balloon amount when it comes due. Oh, oh! So here are some ways to deal with that.

Refinance the property

The first recourse for an owner who wants to keep the property is to refinance either the property itself or another property in the portfolio. This is a good approach as long as financing conditions are favorable. If conditions are not favorable, other approaches will need to be considered.

Sell the property

If the owner does not care to own the property any longer, they can sell it and have the sale pay off the loan. Or they can sell another property to pay off the loan. If conditions are not favorable for selling, again, other approaches will need to be considered. Additionally, income taxes will likely be involved in any sale that takes place.

Renegotiate with the lender

This is not an ideal approach because the borrower is negotiating from an inferior position. The lender has the upper hand because they can always foreclose. So the borrower should offer the lender a monetary inducement for an extension, either a fee, an increase in interest, or payment amount, or both. But it gets the job done. Unless the lender says no!

Protective note terms

The best way for a borrower to protect themselves from becoming in an uncomfortable position is to negotiate protective terms in the note in the first place. One might be called a rollover clause or an extension. Here, for example, the borrower gets a time extension, say two years, for a 2 percent interest rate increase. This must be written in the note as one of its terms.

Another approach is to convert the note into an amortizing one when the balloon payment is due. Again, these terms need to be negotiated when the note is written and included with the other terms. In some cases, lenders do not need a cash payoff and enjoy receiving reliable note payments from a proven borrower. This primarily applies to private lenders.

Bring in a cash partner

If the above approaches aren't working, the borrower can bring in a cash partner. This basically involves selling a partial interest in the property for cash to pay off the balloon. An escrow is recommended with title insurance, and an attorney should draw up an agreement between the parties, who might not be familiar with each other.

Return the property to the lender

This is the least-desirable alternative in most cases. It involves giving up. If it's going to be done, it needs to be done right, with an escrow, deed with a deed in lieu of foreclosure recitation, title insurance, and transfer of any rents and deposits back to the lender. The lender should cancel the note and return the original to the borrower. The lender should also record a full reconveyance in the escrow to clear the title.

File bankruptcy

This is an alternative, but a risky one. The day a bankruptcy is filed, a thirty-day automatic stay of all collection actions is established. After thirty days, the lender can file a relief from stay motion to foreclose on the property. There is a hearing, and in the case of homeowners, the bankruptcy judge will usually urge the parties to work something out. In the case of investors, the sympathy factor is usually low because investors are considered to have resources and several years to handle the balloon. The lender is due the money, the judge is likely to rule (i.e., you lose!). If you are selling or refinancing to handle the balloon, filing bankruptcy can stall the foreclosure. See a bankruptcy attorney well in advance to plan this tactic.

Conclusion

A balloon payment is one of those things that is not a problem until it becomes a problem. It is best to deal with it up front, in initial negotiations, when the note is originated. During the term of the note, keep working to pay it off. If the due date comes and the payoff funds are not in hand, find expert help. You're going to need it.

Chapter 13

Partnering for Profits

The situation today

A large number of real estate investors and would-be investors live in high-priced markets. Large cash down payments are necessary to make a purchase, and even more cash is required to achieve a positive cash flow. This can be discouraging.

One alternative that many in this position consider is turnkey investing, usually in rental houses in distant locations with local real estate support. This involves locations, companies, persons, and properties that are not familiar, and which might, or might not, work out. For sure, the investor has only limited control over their investing fate. Then if a problem arises, the investor has to jump in to right the situation to protect their investment. Passive investing, this is not.

Investing locally with partners

It is not necessary for an investor to send their money thousands of miles to unfamiliar people to invest for them in unfamiliar neighborhoods with properties of uncertain condition and rental prospects. It is definitely possible to invest locally in high-priced properties with a high degree of control by the use of partners.

Three kinds of partners

There are three kinds of partners: 1) a money partner, 2) the seller as a partner, and 3) the tenant as a partner. In each case, the approach is to set up the transaction so that the partner contributes in such a way that the investor profits and the partner receives their benefit from the arrangement.

Partnering with a money partner

The principle here is for the money partner to bring in the funds necessary to make the purchase and set up a reserve to ensure success. There are four investing structures that are attractive based on the interests of the parties:

1)   Limited partnership (LP)
2)   Joint venture (JV)
3)   Tenants in common (TIC)
4)   Limited liability corporation (LLC)

The partnership should be designed so that the money partner receives about an 8 percent annual cash return plus an equity kicker upon liquidation of the investment. The investor needs to provide for themselves as well, even if it means profiting only at the end. Obviously, the better the deal, the more the investor will profit and be able to compensate the money partner. Investors are encouraged to use a real estate attorney to draw up customized documents for the partnership rather than doing it themselves on the cheap with Internet documents. This is not a place to economize! (Hint: You can draw up Internet documents, then have an attorney review them. That should save some money.)

As an example, 3 brothers pooled their funds to purchase a 3-bedroom, 2-bath rental house near Oakland for an LLC that they had created. They put down $178,750 (25 percent) on a purchase price of $715,000, with a new 30-year first loan of $536,250 (75 percent) at 3.1 percent. They paid market price, but the house was being sold by a retiring corporate facilities manager for a national company who had maintained and upgraded it impeccably. They rented it for $3,500 per month. Their overall return is 2.7 percent on their down payment, but since all 3 brothers are in the top federal and California income tax brackets, and starter homes in the Bay Area appreciate strongly, and will for the long term, the brothers will see a nice after-tax return.

Partnering with the seller

There are two major occasions of partnering with sellers. The first is when builder/developers or sophisticated investors enter into a joint venture with the owner of developable land. Typically, the owner contributes the land while the investor obtains the necessary financing, performs the construction, and does the marketing. Then the parties split the profit according to their joint venture agreement. This is a sophisticated partnering method.

The more accessible partnering method with an owner/seller of a property is to use a lease option. Here, the buyer/lessee leases the property on agreed terms and simultaneously negotiates an option to purchase the property in the future at an agreed price and terms. Usually, the buyer/optionee pays some option consideration for the right to purchase during the term of the lease. This is paid either up front or on top of the monthly lease payment. It is important to keep the lease and the option separate but attached because judges in disputes have been known to interpret the documentation unfavorably to the investor. Advice from local real estate counsel is important initially when employing your first lease option. Online and realtor forms can be used, but an attorney should review the first one.

Another accessible partnering method is to negotiate a shared appreciation mortgage (SAM) to be carried back by the seller as owner financing. The idea here is to structure the note such that positive cash flow to the investor is the result. The seller is usually given some cash flow, but not a lot. Then the seller participates in the profit when the property is eventually sold or refinanced. This works well with motivated sellers in high-priced areas. Again, legal advice is recommended for the first time.

Partnering with the tenant

The first method where the tenant is essentially a partner is to use a lease option, to sell this time, rather than to buy. The idea here is to use the lessee's/optionee's option consideration to help pay for the purchase of the property. It can be used as part of the monthly loan payment or as part of the down payment. Either way, since it is not a rental security deposit, it will never need to be refunded.

A second method of partnering with a tenant is known as equity sharing. Here, the parties purchase the property together on the market. One party, the resident co-owner (RCO), resides in the property, maintains it, usually makes the entire loan payment, pays taxes and insurance, and might get the income tax benefits. Those are negotiable, as are the percentage of ownership. The IRS allows taxes to be allocated as the parties decide, as long as they are deducted only once. The investor co-owner (ICO) typically makes the down payment and pays the purchase closing costs. This is all done with extensive documentation, but it is particularly useful for helping first-time buyers get started while allowing investors a high-yield, relatively passive investment. The author represented one unmarried engineer who set up seven of these to help his relatives get started in homeownership while he grew his retirement plan.

Getting started

This topic presents nine different methods for investing with partners in high-priced markets. It is not necessary to wire funds out of state in order to make a profit. Find an expert in the application of these, and get started!

Chapter 14

Buying Real Estate Using Real Property, Personal Property, and Personal Services

Alternatives to cash

Real estate is commonly purchased using cash for a down payment or for the full purchase price. People rarely think of trying something else. This topic presents three other ways to buy properties.

Real and personal property

According to Investopedia, "Real property is the land, everything permanently attached to it, and all of the interests, benefits, and rights inherent in its ownership." You can think of mineral rights, for example. Investopedia says, "Personal property is a class of property that can include any asset other than real estate." Examples are stocks, a vehicle, jewelry, a stamp collection, and so on.

Buying with real property trading

This approach involves trading in a piece of real property as a down payment on other real estate. An example would be if a seller would accept your vacant lakefront lot as a down payment on their eight-unit apartment building.

This is called trading. It is not exchanging as an Internal Revenue Code (IRC) Section 1031 Tax-Deferred Exchange. There is no relationship.

How trading is done

Four aspects of the transaction need to be dealt with are as follows:

No. 1: Values need to be established. This can be done by both parties simply agreeing on values of the trades as part of the negotiations or appraisals can be obtained. If the buyer is getting a new loan on the apartments, that lender will require an appraisal. They will probably want an independent valuation of the lakefront lot as well.

No. 2: Financing. The new loan on the apartments will need to be negotiated with prospective lenders. Additionally, there might be a loan on the land, usually private, that would need to be assumed, taken subject to, or paid off.

No. 3: Conditions. Each property's condition needs to be examined. Residential-type inspections can be done on the apartments. Land-type investigations such as easements, buildability, utilities access, etc., can be done for the lot. Any necessary repairs or other adjustments can be made once the reports are in.

No. 4: Equities. These need to add up and balance. One or another party might need to do some owner-carryback financing, or adjustments in equities can be made using cash.

Much of the purchase agreement will be standardized. However, the down payment term will be customized. Here is an example: "Buyer to trade in a vacant lakefront lot at Clearlake, California, described more particularly in Addendum #1, and valued at $60,000.00, as the down payment."

Buying with personal property

Submitting personal property as a down payment, or even as partial consideration along with cash, on a piece of real estate is similar to the process described above. The steps are the same. The parties can agree on a value for the personal property, accumulate supporting evidence, or hire a specialized appraiser. For example, Kelly Blue Book (KBB) can be used for a motor vehicle.

The author has seen a gorgeous wooden 1930s motor yacht used for a down payment. Vehicles, motorhomes, promissory notes, gemstones, jewelry, securities, shop equipment, and antiques are some examples. Use your imagination! The author once gave an unfinished rolltop desk that he bought on a VISA card for a down payment on two rental houses with seller financing. See if you can beat that!

Buying with professional or personal services

A third way of buying is with professional or personal services. Examples here are a dentist installing implants, a plumber doing repiping, and a landscaper redoing a front yard.

Example wording might be as follows: "Dr. Malcolm and Mrs. Carie Brightbite will provide dental implants to seller based on the attached Dental Services Contract valued at $60,000.00 as a down payment on the subject property."

Using this approach has an added benefit. The dentist, plumber, and landscaper provide their services at their cost, but they get credit at a retail value. They are making a profit on their service or getting a discount on the property, depending on how you want to look at it.

Dealing with lenders

In these transactions, it will be unproductive to go to major lenders because they package their loans into securities and sell them to replenish their funding supply. Local banks and credit unions are worth a try because they retain and service their loans. Having, or opening, an account, there should help. You can be sure that they will want appraisals and inspections for their loan file.

Your best bet is private lenders. Investors are constantly seeking yield in alternatives to banks. Private lending is booming as a result. An online search will produce plenty of lenders for you to interview. Not everyone will lend to you, but some will. They need to put their money out, after all.

Advanced techniques

Here are a couple techniques for readers who want to become a wheeler dealer in cashless acquisition of real estate.

No. 1: Craigslist

> Try placing two ads on Craigslist under Barter (free) and under Real Estate Wanted. Make them marketing campaigns, which means refine your ads and see what works. You might get a deal or two per year, but at five dollars per month, you can just keep the ads running. You'll meet some real characters too!

No. 2: Barter organizations

> See what is available in your area. Sometimes you can barter for an item that you can successfully use to buy a piece of real estate!

Getting started

Acquiring real estate in these ways is challenging due to the creative thinking that is required. It is also fun to be in these kinds of negotiations. The author was an observer when two wheeler dealers were discussing the value of a 3-carat diamond that was being offered. It happened to be muddy brown, like a river in springtime. The offeror wanted a thirty-thousand-dollar credit for it. The offeree said he would take it in at ten thousand dollars. My twenty-one-year-old assistant whispered to me, "It's worth only four thousand dollars, Bruce." I replied, "I know, Kristi, but they're having fun!"

So inventory your personal property and tradable skills. Get started!

Chapter 15

Finding Opportunities

What to look for

The fortunate and exciting thing about creative financing is the large variety of transactions where it can be applied. Here's what to look for:

1) Properties that have gotten away from their owners. These would be visibly run-down or with high vacancies, evictions, preforeclosures, tax delinquencies, etc.
2) Free and clear properties that have no loan. Since the seller has abundant equity, these are excellent candidates for seller financing, even with no down payment.
3) High-equity properties that have a loan. These are similar to no. 2, except a little less flexible because the loan has to be dealt with. There are plenty of methods for this in this book.
4) Low-equity properties are more restricted in what you can do, but usually there are a lot more of them. This is the time to skip through them quickly and play the numbers game.
5) Underwater properties are ones where the loan(s) exceed the value of the property. These are ideal for subject-to purchases, and sellers are often eager to give them away if you will pay their closing costs. You need to make sure the deal is financially sound, however.

Where to look

Sources of properties (25) are as follows:

1) Absentee owners
2) Bank real estate owned (REOs)
3) Bankruptcy filings
4) Building code violations
5) Community land banks (mostly rust belt)
6) Damaged properties (e.g., fire, flood)
7) Delinquent property taxes
8) Divorce
9) Neighborhood searching—"Driving for dollars"
10) Expired MLS listings
11) Fire departments
12) For sale by owners (FSBOs)
13) Hard-money lender repossessions
14) Housing and Urban Development (HUD) foreclosures
15) Mobile home dealer trade-ins
16) Nonprofit/Charities donations of real estate
17) Preforeclosures
18) Private money lender repossessions
19) Probate executors/administrators
20) Property wholesalers
21) Tired landlords (e.g., evictions)
22) US Department of Agriculture (USDA) foreclosures
23) US Treasury Department IRS auctions
24) US Treasury confiscated real estate auctions
25) Veterans Administration (VA) foreclosures

How to look

Marketing tools and methods (49) are as follows:

1) Ads in state press associations
2) Attend garage sales

3) Attend investor seminars
4) Attend open houses to buy
5) Attend real estate auctions
6) Bandit signs
7) Billboards
8) Business cards
9) Business brochure
10) Business card/flyer in real estate books at bookstore
11) Business card/flyer in real estate books in libraries
12) Call For Rent signs
13) Car signs and bumper stickers
14) Classified ads (e.g., Craigslist)
15) Cultivate Realtors
16) Direct mail
17) Door hangers
18) Door knocking
19) E-book (author is you)
20) E-letter to your sphere of influence (SOI)
21) Farm low-income areas
22) Flyers
23) Google AdWords
24) Hiring "Bird Dogs (see below)
25) Join Chamber of Commerce
26) Join Rotary Club
27) Join Toastmasters
28) Leave cards/flyers at nursing/retirement homes
29) Letters to owners
30) License plate frames
31) Local magazine ads
32) Mail to trustees of trusts
33) Network events (expos, meet-ups, REIAs)
34) Online searching auction sites (e.g., www.auction.com)
35) Online magazines
36) Online real estate sites (e.g., Zillow, Redfin)
37) Phone canvassing
38) Place ads in worship bulletins

39) Post videos on YouTube ™
40) Publish a book
41) Postcards to owners
42) Restaurant and bar tables (business cards)
43) Set up a website
44) Search eBay
45) Search Loopnet
46) Search Multiple Listing Service (MLS)
47) Search www.Realtor.com
48) Search Crexi
49) Social media

Opportunities can also come by way of referrals from others. One source is bird dogs, people who are out in the field much of the time. Another source is professionals who learn about properties in the course of their work. These two sources are listed below, and they come with the warning that some states might regulate the payment of referral fees. For example, California restricts its real estate licensees to paying referral fees only to other licensees, and not to the public. Unlicensed people are not restricted in California. So check your state's regulations about referral fees.

Bird dogs in the field (25) are as follows:

1) Apartment leasing reps
2) Charity employees
3) City bus drivers
4) Drycleaners
5) Exterminators
6) Funeral directors
7) Garbage collectors
8) Hair dressers and nail parlors
9) House cleaners
10) Junk dealers
11) Landscapers and gardeners
12) Mail carriers

13) Mold removal companies
14) Moving companies
15) Notaries
16) Nursing home employees
17) Pizza delivery drivers
18) Legal process servers
19) Property preservation companies
20) Rental car employees
21) Security guards
22) Storage companies
23) Taxi/Uber, Lyft drivers
24) UPS, FedEx, UPS drivers
25) Utility workers

A bird dog agreement can be found on the Internet. That keeps it businesslike.

Referrals from professionals (21) are as follows:

1) Accountants
2) Appraisers
3) Attorneys (various)
4) Bail bonders
5) Bank employees
6) Bookkeepers
7) Closing attorneys
8) Doctors and dentists
9) Financial advisors
10) Homeowners associations (HoA)
11) Home inspectors
12) Insurance agents and brokers
13) Marriage counselors
14) Mortgage brokers and bankers
15) New home builders
16) Property managers
17) Real estate brokers and agents

18) Religious and spiritual leaders
19) Relocation (RELO) companies
20) Resume services
21) Title and escrow company employees

The next chapter, chapter 16, presents how to craft offers using creative financing.

Chapter 16

Crafting Creative Offers

Application

Many readers here will no doubt have experience with offers, writing them, issuing them, and receiving them. They might have brokers, agents, and attorneys who represent them. These readers need not spend much time on this chapter. Mostly, they should refer to other chapters for ideas how to buy or sell creatively. Always refer to chapter 4 about note terms when proposing seller financing.

This chapter covers the steps to preparing a creative offer using the purchase and sale agreement in appendix A and the attachments in appendix B.

Step 1. Read appendix A. Think about each of the terms. Are there any that don't apply or you want to delete? Can you think of anything to add? Under Terms of Purchase (section 2), you have to choose because some are mutually exclusive. You can't use them all. That's how you craft an offer.

Step 2. Now consider addendum no. 1 in appendix B, along with chapter 4. Choose your note terms to go in your offer from appendix A.

Step 3. Addendum no. 2 includes some minimum disclosure requirements for California. Whatever state you are in, you need to research the required disclosures there and produce your own addendum to be negotiated and signed.

Step 4. Addendum no. 3 needs to be completed and signed. If buyer to seller are at the kitchen table, this addendum probably would not be necessary.

Step 5. Addendum no. 4 concerns any homeowner's association. If it applies, you need to include it with your offer. Additionally, since state laws differ in this area, you need to check requirements for the state where you are transacting.

Step 6. Addendum no. 5 applies if you are transacting land. Otherwise, you can ignore it.

Note: These are the forms that the author has used repeatedly. The idea here is for you to use these for ideas to develop your own set. A competent attorney, broker, or agent can help you with that.

Chapter 17

Conclusion
The Creative Mindset

It takes a while to become proficient implementing the concepts presented in this book. Your patience is rewarded when you discover that you can own a lot more properties by using creative financing than you ever could by using cash. After all, your cash resources are finite. Your creative resources are not.

So after using chapter 15 to locate opportunities, you have to look at them a certain way—that is, with a creative mindset. You have to become a transaction engineer, looking at the opportunity several, various ways. When you conclude the best way, then you put the structure on it, covered in chapter 16.

And that's how creative financing works. You put the structure on it.

Appendix A

Purchase and Sale Agreement

Date:______________, 20______, at ____________________, California

Receipt for Deposit:

1.   Received from Buyer(s) ____
and/or assigns, $___________, evidenced by ___________________, payable to
_________________________________, to be held undeposited until acceptance
of this offer, as a deposit toward the purchase of property situated in the City of
___________________, County of ___________________, State of ______________,
described as ___________________________, APN: _________________

Terms of Purchase

2.   Buyer to pay the purchase price as follows:

   2.1. Cash payment through escrow, including deposit $___________.

   2.2. Buyer to obtain a first/second loan on terms acceptable to Buyer, at
         Buyer's expense $___________.

   2.3. Buyer to take title subject to an existing loan with___________________
         under its present terms and conditions $___________.

       2.3.1 Loan balance differences per loan statements to be adjusted into
              carryback note.

       2.3.2. Impound account, if any, to be transferred to Buyer without charge.

   2.4. Buyer to execute in favor of Seller a carryback note $___________ with
         terms according to Addendum #1—Note Terms.

   2.5. Sale by Land Contract: The purchase price shall be paid in accordance with
         the attached Land Contract, which is incorporated in here by reference.

Total purchase price: $___________

3.   Property Included

   3.1. Fixtures and fittings attached to the property include, but are not limited
         to: window shades, blinds, light fixtures, plumbing fixtures, curtain
         rods, wall-to-wall carpeting, draperies, hardware, antennas, air coolers
         and conditioners, trees, shrubs, mailboxes, and other similar items.

3.2. The sale shall also include all personal property, except:

____.

3.3. Unless specifically excluded, all other items will be included, whether or not affixed to the property or structures. Seller expressly warrants that property, improvements, building or structures, appliances, roof, plumbing, heating, and/or ventilation systems are in good and working order. This clause shall survive closing of title.

3.4. Seller to maintain the property in good condition until possession is delivered.

4. Acceptance and Performance

4.1. This offer expires unless accepted in writing within _____ calendar days after date, and acceptance is personally delivered, faxed, or emailed to Buyer within this period.

4.2. In the event Buyer is unable to arrange financing as agreed by the date scheduled for closing, Buyer may terminate this agreement, with buyer's deposit promptly refunded.

4.3. Any termination of this agreement shall be by written Notice of Cancellation, timely delivered to the other party, or the other party's broker, with instructions to Escrow to return all instruments and funds to the parties depositing them.

4.4. Should Buyer breach this agreement, Buyer's monetary liability to Seller (i.e., "liquidated damages") is limited to the deposit receipted in Section 1.

4.5. Both parties reserve their rights to assign and agree to cooperate in conducting an IRS Sec. 1031 Tax-deferred Exchange within this transaction, on either party's written notice.

5. Property Conditions

Seller shall deliver to Buyer the following at Seller's expense:

5.1. A structural pest control report and certification of clearance of corrective measures (i.e., "Section I" items).

5.2. A property inspection report by a licensed property inspector showing the land and improvements to be free of material defects.

5.3. A septic system report by a licensed septic system contractor certifying that the septic tank, pump, and leach field are in good working order, and that any necessary repairs have been made, and the tank does not need pumping.

5.4. Certification by a licensed water testing laboratory certifying that the well supplying the property meets water potability standards.

5.5. Certification by a licensed well contractor stating that the well supplying the property produces a minimum flow of _____ gallons per minute.

6.   Risk of Loss

The risk of loss by destruction or damage to the property by fire or otherwise prior to closing is that of the Seller. If all or a substantial portion of the improvements on the property are destroyed or damaged, this agreement shall be voidable at the option of the Buyer, and the earnest money deposit shall be promptly refunded.

7.   Real Estate Taxes, Rents, Deposits, Insurance

Real estate taxes assessed against the property shall be prorated through the date of closing. Rents, if any, shall be likewise prorated, and all tenant deposits and prepaid rents shall be transferred to the Buyer. Seller shall arrange for Estoppel Certificates to be completed and signed by tenants. Existing casualty insurance shall be canceled or prorated as agreed by the parties.

8.   Possession

    8.1.   Seller shall deliver possession of the property free of all debris and in "broom clean" condition at closing. Buyer has the right to do a "final walk through," or send a representative, prior to closing, and to take any pictures desired.

    8.2.   Buyer shall be entitled to a door key and entitled to access to show the property to partners, lenders, inspectors, contractors, tenants, and investors.

    8.3.   Buyer may place an appropriate sign on the property prior to closing, and advertise its availability for rent, sale, or investment.

9.   General Conditions

    9.1.   This agreement shall become effective as of the date of the last signature.

    9.2.   This agreement may be executed in counterparts, by fax, and by email.

    9.3.   The parties hereto agree that this is the entire agreement between them, and that there are no other agreements, oral or written.

    9.4.   This agreement shall be binding upon the heirs, personal representatives, successors and assigns of both Buyer and Seller.

    9.5.   This agreement shall be interpreted and enforced in accordance with the laws of the State of ___________________________.

10.   Title

Seller shall provide Buyer promptly after acceptance of this offer, at Seller's expense, a preliminary title report or abstract of title, as a prelude to issuance of an owner's policy of title insurance. If the abstract fails to show insurable title vested in Seller, a reasonable time shall be permitted to correct title defects. In the event such corrections cannot be made, the parties shall cancel this agreement, and Buyer's deposit shall be promptly refunded. Seller shall convey title to Buyer at closing by a good and sufficient grant or general warranty deed free and clear of all liens and encumbrances except as otherwise provided in this offer, and subject to easements, zoning, and restrictions of record.

11. Closing Conditions

    11.1. _________ to select settlement agent/Escrow and title insurer.

    11.2. Parties to hand Escrow all documents required by the title insurer, lenders, or other third parties to this transaction at least five days prior to the scheduled date of closing.

    11.3. Closing is scheduled for _________________________.

    11.4. Seller to provide Buyer with an inventory and Bill of Sale for any personal property being transferred, including any owner's or operating manuals for the same.

12. Closing Costs

    12.1. Escrow Fee shall be paid _____________________________.

    12.2. Owner's Title Policy shall be paid _________________________.

    12.3. (Any) Lender's Title Policy shall be paid by Buyer.

    12.4. County Transfer Tax shall be paid _________________________.

    12.5. (Any) City Transfer Tax shall be paid _________________________.

13. Addenda

The following Addenda are attached to this agreement, and are incorporated herein.

    13.1. Addendum #1: Note Terms

    13.2. Addendum #2: Required Disclosures

    13.3. Addendum #3: Broker and Attorney

    13.4. Addendum #4: Owners' Association

    13.5. Addendum #5: Land Purchase

14. Buyer's Signature

_______________________   _______________________

      Buyer   Date

15. Seller's Acceptance

The undersigned Seller(s) accepts this Purchase Agreement.

_______________________   _______________________

      Seller   Seller

_______________________   _______________________

      Date   Date

Seller's Acceptance is subject to a Counteroffer dated _______________.

End of Purchase Agreement

Appendix B

Addendum No. 1
Note Terms

This is an Addendum to that Purchase Agreement by and between
________________________________, Buyer, and _________________________________,
Seller(s), dated_________________________________, 20________, regarding that property at
____.

1. Request for Notice of Delinquency to senior lenders.

2. Unsecured

3. Late charge

4. Due on sale

5. Assumption

6. Balloon patment

7. Option to extend

8. Interest only

9. Zero interest/principal only

10. Deferred interest

11. Skip a payment

12. Substitution of collateral

13. Right of first refusal

14. No repayment penalty

15. Prepayment discount

16. Shared appreciation

17. Graduated payments

Appendix B (continued)

Addendum No. 2
Required Disclosures

This is an Addendum to that Purchase Agreement by and between
______________________, Buyer, and ______________________,
Seller(s), dated ______________________, 20______, regarding that property at
____.

1. Buyer acknowledges receipt of a booklet and Seller and disclosures regarding:

    (a) *Environmental Hazards: a Guide for Homeowners, Landlords, and Tenants* (on all one-to-four units),

    (b) *Protect Your Family from Lead in Your Home* (on all pre-1978, one-to-four units),

    (c) *The Homeowner's Guide to Earthquake Safety* (on all pre-1960, one-to-four units).

2. Buyer acknowledges receipt of seller's *Property Condition Disclosure* dated ______________________ prior to signing this Purchase Agreement. OR, Buyer acknowledges that no disclosure statement is required due to ______________________.

3. Seller to provide Buyer with a *Seller's Natural Hazard Disclosure Statement* to be handed to Buyer upon acceptance for Buyer's review, and within ten days, Buyer may terminate this agreement based on a reasonable disapproval of hazards disclosed by the statement and unknown to buyer prior to acceptance.

______________________ ______________________
Buyer   Date

______________________ ______________________
Seller   Date

______________________ ______________________
Seller   Date

Addendum No. 3
Broker and Attorney

This is an Addendum to that Purchase Agreement by and between
_______________________________, Buyer, and _______________________________,
Seller(s), dated _______________________________, 20_______, regarding that property at
____.

1. Seller(s) have employed _______________________________

   as their Listing Broker in this transaction and will compensate them according to their separate Listing Agreement.

2. Seller(s) have retained

   ____

   as their attorneys-at-law in this transaction and will compensate them according to their separate Retainer Agreement.

3. Buyer is a licensed Real Estate Agent in the State of California, who is purchasing the subject property for investment as a principal. Buyer expects no real estate commission from the Seller, and the Buyer has no agency or fiduciary relationship with the Seller(s).

_______________________________   _______________________________

Buyer   Date

_______________________________   _______________________________

Seller   Date

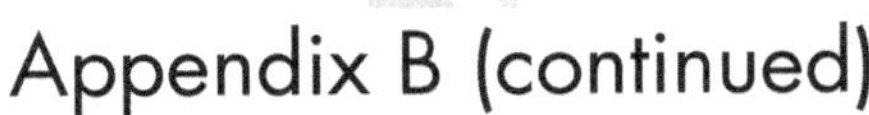

Addendum No. 4
Owners' Association

This is an Addendum to that Purchase Agreement by and between
_______________________________, Buyer, and _______________________________,
Seller(s), dated _______________________________, 20________, regarding that property at
____.

1. The sale is conditioned on Buyer's receipt at Seller's expense, within ten days, and Buyer's written approval of, each of the following Owners' Association documents:

   Articles of Incorporation   By-Laws

   Conditions, Covenants, and Restrictions (CC & R's)

   Operating Rules and Regulations   Reserves

   Restrictions (e.g., age, pets, rental, usage)

   Collection and Lien Enforcement Policy   Budget

   CPA's Review and Certification   Insurance Policy

   Regular and Special Assessments   Financial Statement

   Any pending or anticipated claim or litigation by or against the HOA

   Location and number of designated parking and storage spaces

   Copies of the most recent six months HOA minutes for regular and special meetings

2. No association claims for defects or changes in regular or special assessments are pending or anticipated. Current monthly assessment is $_______________________.

3. Seller is not in violation of CC & R's, except

   ____.

4. There is no litigation pending except

   ____.

5. Seller to pay association document fee. Buyer to pay association transfer fee.

6. Within ten days of Buyer's receipt of the association documents, Buyer may terminate this transaction based upon reasonable disapproval of the documents.

___________________	___________________
Buyer	Date
___________________	___________________
Seller	Seller
___________________	___________________
Date	Date

Appendix B (final)

Addendum No. 5
Land Purchase

This is an Addendum to that Purchase Agreement by and between
______________________________, Buyer, and ______________________________,
Seller(s), dated ______________________________, 20______, regarding that property at
____.

Seller Documentation and Disclosure:

Seller to provide to Buyer, in writing, the following information:

1. LEGAL PROCEEDINGS: any lawsuits by or against Seller, threatening or affecting the Property.

2. AGRICULTURE USE: whether the property is subject to any restrictions for agricultural use.

3. DEED RESTRICTIONS: any deed restrictions or obligations.

4. ENDANGERED SPECIES: presence of endangered, threatened, "candidate" species, or wetlands on the Property.

5. ENVIRONMENTAL HAZARDS: any substances, materials, or products that may be an environmental hazard including, but not limited to, asbestos, formaldehyde, radon gas, lead-based paint, fuel or chemical storage tanks, and contaminated soil or water on the property.

6. COMMON WALLS: any features of the property shared in common with adjoining landowners.

7. LANDLOCKED: the absence of legal or physical access to the property.

8. EASEMENTS/ENCROACHMENTS: any encroachments or easements or similar matters that may affect the property.

9. SOIL FILL: any fill (compacted or otherwise) or abandoned mining operation on the Property.

10. SOIL PROBLEMS: any slippage, sliding, flooding, drainage, grading, or other soil problems.

11. EARTHQUAKE DAMAGE: major damage to the property or any of the structures from fire, earthquake, floods, or landslides.

12. ZONING ISSUES: any zoning violations, non-conforming uses, or violations of "setbacks" requirements.

13. Neighborhood problems: any neighborhood noise problems, or other nuisances (e.g., odors, traffic).

14. MANUFACTURED HOME PLACEMENT: conditions that may affect the ability to place and use a manufactured home on the property.

15. UTILITIES AND SERVICES: availability, costs, restrictions and location of utilities and services, including but not limited to, sewerage, sanitation, septic and leach lines, water, electricity, gas, telephone, cable TV, and drainage.

16. SURVEY, PLANS, AND ENGINEERING DOCUMENTS: copies of surveys, places, specifications, and engineering documents, if any.

17. PERMITS: copies of all permits and approvals obtained from any government of entity for any purpose.

Appendix C

Resource Library
For Leases and Options

1) Conti, Peter, and David Finkel. 2002. *Making Big Money Investing in Real Estate.* Chicago, Illinois: Dearborn Financial Publishing Inc.

2) Fisher, Steven D. 2007. *Real Estate Options.* Ocala, Florida: Atlantic Publishing Group Inc.

3) Gardiner, Richard R., and Macy, Linda S., JD. 1984. *Creating Wealth with Options.* San Ramon, California: Impact Publishing Co.

4) Ham, Bill. 2021. *Creative Cash.* Jake & Gino Presents.

5) Little, James F., MBA, CCIM. 1991, 1995. *Lease-Options in Today's Real Estate Market.* Self-published.

6) Lucier, Thomas J. 2005. *How to Make Money with Real Estate Options.* Hoboken, New Jersey: John Wiley & Sons.

7) Lowry, Albert. Copyright 1984 est. *Make Money through Lease Options.* The Lowry Group.

8) Patton, Wendy. 2005. *Investing in Real Estate with Lease-Options and Subject-To Deals.* Hoboken, New Jersey: John Wiley & Sons Inc.

9) Pellerin, Jim. 2019. *Real Estate Investing with Lease-Options,* Realty Investment Seminars & Education. Self-Published.

10) Prefontaine, Chris. 2020. *Real Estate on Your Terms, Revised Edition.* Charleston, South Carolina: Advantage.

11) Prefontaine, Chris. 2021. *Deal Structure Overtime,* Wicked Smart Books.

12) Price, Oliver Ray. 1978. *High Leverage Real Estate Investments*. Englewood Cliffs, New Jersey: Prentice-Hall Inc.
13) Schaub, John. 1987. *Lease-Options*. Sarasota, Florida: Pro-Serve Corp.

Appendix D

Resource Books

These books come from the author's library, which began in 1980. The author is a leverage mechanic who has purchased over three hundred properties for zero down and another one hundred or so with high leverage. So that's the kind of resources being offered here.

Some of these books can be found, used, online, such as at Amazon. Those by Dr. Al Lowry can be searched at his website. Of course, there are current books on much of this material as well. Anyone with the desire can build up a knowledge base of high-leverage property acquisition if they apply themselves.

1. Allen, Robert G. 1983. *Creating Wealth.* New York: Simon & Schuster.
2. Allen, Richard J. 1982. *How to Write a Nothing Down Offer.* Provo, Utah: The Allen Group Inc.
3. Allen, Robert G. 1982. *Nothing Down.* New York: Simon & Schuster.
4. Beckley, Ed. 1980. *125 Irresistible Purchase Offers.* Fairfield, Iowa: Midwest Financial Publications.
5. Beckley, Ed. 1982. *No Down Payment Formulas.* Roseville, California: No Down Payment Institute.
6. Cook, Wade. 1998. *101 Ways to Buy Real Estate Without Cash,* 1998. S. Seattle, Washington: Lighthouse Publishing Group Inc.
7. Cook, Wade. 1983. *How to Build a Real Estate Money Machine.* Orem, Utah: Investment & Tax Publications Inc.

8. Cook, Wade. 1985. *Real Wealth*. Tempe, Arizona: Regency Books.

9. Cummings, Jack. 1982. *Cashless Investing in Real Estate*. New York: Playboy Press.

10. Del Dotto, Dave. 1982. *101 Purchase Offers Sellers Can't Resist*. San Ramon, California: Impact Publishing Co.

11. Farrell, Mike. 1984. *Million Dollar Formula*. Impact Publishing Co.

12. Glubetich, Dave. 1980. *Double Your Money in Real Estate Every 2 Years*. Impact Publishing Co.

13. Hall, Sam. 1983. *Positive Solutions to Negative Cash Flows*. Provo, Utah: The Allen Group Inc.

14. Hebestreet, John. 1984. *How to Write an Offer To Purchase Real Estate*. Impact Publishing Co.

15. Lowry, Albert J., PhD. 1982. *58 No Money Down Techniques*. Westlake Village, California: The Lowry Group.

16. Lowry, Albert J., PhD. 1984. *197 Creative Financing Techniques*. The Lowry Group.

17. Lowry, Albert J., PhD. 1982. *How You Can Become Financially Independent Investing in Real Estate*. New York: Simon & Schuster.

18. Lowry, Albert J., PhD. *How to Make Your Money Grow (Using Notes)*. Copyright and Publisher unknown.

19. Lowry, Albert J., PhD. 1984. *Positive Cash Flow Made Easy*. The Lowry Group.

20. Price, Oliver Ray. 1978. *High Leverage Real Estate Investments*. Englewood Cliffs, New Jersey: Prentice-Hall Inc.

21. Stephen, Mitch. 2015. *My Life & 1,000 Houses (200+ Ways to Find Bargain Properties)*. Mitch Stephen (self-published)

22. Zick, Bernard. 1986. *How to Buy a House Using S.A.M (Shared-Appreciation Mortgage)*. Solana Beach, California.

About the Author

Bruce Kellogg has been a realtor and investor in California for forty-five years. He purchased about 350 investment properties for himself, mostly with high leverage and tax-deferred exchanges. In the process, he made three fortunes and experienced three real estate downturns since 1980. He has transacted about 550 properties for clients, creating fortunes for several.

Mr. Kellogg has published about fifty articles in three national real estate wealth-building magazines. His clients and readers occasionally refer to him as a real estate wizard. This is his second book sharing his accumulated experience and his wisdom.